DEDI

This book is dedicated to my adopted father, Wayne, who unfortunately, passed away before publication. One of the most hardworking, selfless, loving, giving, and forgiving men I have ever been honoured to know. He loved my idea for my book, and supported it 100%. He even approved the title for it.

He raised me to be strong and independent, yet soft and nurturing.

Everything I have, am, and have become, is all because one man chose me to be his little girl - his daughter. And I am forever grateful that he is the one I got to call Daddy.

It is also dedicated to my adopted mother, Mary, who has always taught me to challenge myself, give others the benefit of the doubt, and always, no matter what, stay true to myself, and never sell myself short. They both have always supported me, stood by me, and been there whenever I have ever needed them. And, for that, I will be eternally grateful, and my heart will always be full of love for them both.

CONTENTS

ACKNOWLEDGMENTS

I would like to send out a special thanks to my good friend Tammy for doing all my proof reading and editing of this book, as well as Search Trace Locate for assisting me in my search.

This book has been a very long time in the making, after many attempts, re-writes, lost manuscripts, and sleepless nights, so all help and encouragement that has been given to me from family and friends has been greatly appreciated, and I love you all for it.

The craziness is over – for now.

1. BEING AN ADOPTEE – WHAT DOES IT MEAN?

What does it mean to be an adoptee? That's a very good question. And the answer always depends on who you're asking. Some people think that it's just someone that is adopted. Well, if you're an adoptee, you know it's much more than that.

For some, it's a state of being, a state of mind, a way of living, a way of thinking. For others, it's an obsession, a whirling tornado of thoughts, a mind-boggling amount of questions that could crash the world's largest computer server if asked all at once, a roller coaster of emotions, a myriad of mysteries shrouded in deception.

Of course, for some, it's "no big deal", and the thought of being an adoptee rarely crosses their minds as it's nothing they really care to know about, investigate, or live in. They're simply happy being who they are, with the family they're with, no real desire to know anything different, and that's just fine with them.

Some people actually change how they feel about the whole thing over time, with age and wisdom or, sometimes because they spoke to someone, or read something, that gave them have a different outlook or opinion than they first had.

There is nothing wrong with being any of those types of people, or, the type of person you currently are, or were, for that matter. There is nothing wrong with changing your opinion, or outlook on something. Every single adoptee is completely justified in feeling the way they feel. They are entitled to it, they've earned the right to feel exactly how they do. No one can ever tell you that your feelings are wrong. They're feelings, and, more importantly, they're _your_ feelings. You feel the way you feel, and no any one person's feelings are wrong. It's what you do with how you feel that matters, and either keeps or changes your outlook and/or opinions.

Some people have no idea what they feel about it, or why, or what to do about it. And, that is perfectly fine too.

It's very difficult to explain what it's like to be an adoptee, or how it feels. It would be like trying to explain pregnancy or childbirth to someone that has never experienced it. You can explain how everything feels, how your body moves, and stretches, and aches like after a long hard day doing physical labour, or a an intense workout at the gym. You can try to explain how every little shift and movement the baby makes feels like a big bowl of heavy jelly inside your belly undigested. You can explain how labour pains feel like a kick to the crotch, or like a severe round of menstrual cramps.

They may get the general idea of what you're experiencing, or feeling, but, not really know what it's *actually* like. There's a big difference between *understanding* something and *knowing* it.

Unless you're talking to another adoptee, that is.

There are so many of us out there that can have endless conversations about how we feel about being adopted. About how we feel as a person, as an individual, and how we feel emotionally about it, not just mentally.

There is such a myriad of things that go on in an adoptee's mind ranging from the most horrible negative thoughts and emotions, to the most positive and uplifting. It's the biggest mental roller coaster ride in the biggest emotional amusement park on earth, or on any planet for some. For others, it's just another day.

Let's start with the negative thoughts and get those out of the way first.

Adoptees can often have unfavourable feelings of self-doubt and self-worth and often blame themselves for being "unwanted", or "unloved" by the one person that is supposed to love them and want them more than anything in the world - their natural birth mother. The one person they are supposed to be able to bond with, grow with, look up to, love, and be loved by unconditionally. And, for some reason, that never happened. So, they blame themselves.

They may think something is wrong with them, or that they were an ugly baby, or that they would be a burden or a problem for their mothers. They may grow up constantly feeling like there is something so horrible about them, that they that they don't deserve to be loved by someone else, and certainly can't love themselves. They may feel that their new parents adopted them out of sheer pity, and that they only reason they were keeping them around is because they *had* to, not that they really *wanted* to.... When adoptees feel like this, they can't and don't understand that their adopted parents want them because they were specially chosen by them, and loved them. For some adoptees, this can be a very hard mental and emotional obstacle to get past.

Naturally, the first thoughts, either negative or positive, always start with the birth mother, because she is the one that carries you and delivers you. She is the one that makes sure that before you enter the world you're fed, growing properly, developing properly, cared for, and protected.

This is where the feelings of abandonment come into play. From the moment you leave her body and enter the world, you may feel that you've been tossed aside, uncared for, unloved, forgotten, and abandoned. It's hard to understand how any woman can go to all the extremes that she does, only to act so cold and uncaring to just walk away from their child; to leave their baby helpless and alone, with nobody to care for them and to love them. This is why the adoptee may start to feel that there is something wrong with them that could cause any mother to do something like that to their child. Thus, starts the feelings of inadequacy, self-doubt, worthlessness, and for some, despair and depression.

There are some that feel like they just don't belong anywhere, or with anyone. They feel like they just don't fit in anywhere because they aren't from this area, from this family, or even from this life. They feel like they just can't assimilate into their surroundings because they know something just isn't quite right. Something just isn't clicking; they feel it to their very bones and can't explain it. They just don't feel like themselves. or, more accurately, they feel like they are themselves, but like they are someone else entirely at the same time. That's where the feelings of the title of this book come into play. I feel like I'm myself, but I feel like I'm someone else. I'm me, but I'm not.

Now, in comes the battle with positive thoughts.

The adoptee now has two wonderful, doting, giving, caring, and loving parents that have taken them in as their own who help to give the child their sense of belonging, and self-worth. It's a struggle at this point, and can be very confusing with such conflicting feelings. The adoptee struggles to understand how mentally and emotionally two complete strangers can possibly love someone that isn't theirs, someone that doesn't belong to them. Someone that they didn't create, that isn't their own flesh and blood. This is completely understandable, and completely normal.

It's hard for a lot of people that *aren't* adopted to understand how anyone can bring a baby or an older child into their homes and lives in the first place and love it so much without it being their own... being someone else's that they have never known or met.

For some adoptees, this creates a much bigger dilemma. A much bigger battle mentally and emotionally. It can actually cause distrust because they have such a hard time believing that it's true or even possible.

It can take many years before the adoptee can believe, truly believe, that it really is possible and indeed true. That they do matter, are really are loved, cared for, and mean the world to someone that isn't related to them. They find the revelation that someone actually does love them not because they are family - flesh and blood family - and "have to", but because they were specially chosen, specially selected, deeply wanted, and sincerely loved because then can, and choose to.

On the other hand, there are some adoptees that are on the complete opposite end of the spectrum. There are some adoptees that are completely fine with their situations and have no interest in learning anything about their past, their birth family, their history, or their origins.

Some are quite content with the lives and families they have been given and these adoptees have a different mindset. They may feel that they can't possibly miss what they never had so they don't want to search for their birth families because they have no desire to know who they are. This is sometimes combined with anger and resentment. Sometimes the adoptee might not feel like their birth mother and birth families do not have any rights to know anything about the adoptee because they gave up that right along with their parental rights and gave them away to perfect strangers.

This is also perfectly normal for the adoptee to feel.

Sometimes, the adoptee goes through every single one of these emotions, feelings and thoughts at different times. Sometimes there are even feelings, emotions and thoughts that can't be explained, even by the adoptee themselves.

One of the things that I have found for those adoptees that are struggling, what most often comes up are feelings of missing out on something, or even getting angry about the issues. When you grow up as an adoptee, you will often think about the "what-if's" and when this generally causes the anger side of the emotions, these are the people I find feel like they have missed out on something growing up, that they may have felt like they had an unhappy, or unfulfilled childhood. They feel that they are owed an answer by their birth mother as to what happened and why. They get angry if they are denied contact, or have trouble establishing contact or difficulty in finding their birth mothers. They feel that it is their right to have those answers given to them, and that their birth mother or birth family has no right to deny that to them.

Figuring out the missing link, doing the detective work, the searching becomes of primary importance. I have found the majority of people that are "on a mission" as I call it, or "hellbent for answers" are generally the ones that truly feel a sense of lacking, and a sense of missing out. While those that don't feel they lacked for anything are perfectly happy with the way their lives are, and generally, have had a very happy, loving, fulfilling childhood and don't feel like they are missing out on anything. My favourite saying after I had a daughter of my own and she got older, realized my childhood wasn't really as bad as I thought it was when I was in my pre-teens and teens. When I restarted my own search, and was a little wiser my thought was: "If I find my birth mother, great. If not, well, oh well. If she wants to be friends, cool, if not, oh well. I'm not really overly concerned one way or another. It's not like I'm missing out on anything... I have a mom. And, I love my mom. So, I can't really miss what I never had."

And that seems to be the mindset of the majority of the ones that had a good childhood with good, loving parents. They don't feel like anything within themselves was lacking. There is generally a good relationship with their adoptive parents as well, which is why one finds that mind set of ambivalence when it comes to finding birth mothers or families. They don't feel "ripped-off", so to speak.

While this is completely normal and understandable, this perspective often comes as the adoptee becomes older and wiser. Even I started out in my pre-teens and into my very early twenties, with the mindset that my birth mother owed me. If nothing else, she owed me answers that I was entitled to, answers she that she had no right to deny that to me and how dare she not come searching for me the day I turned eighteen! I believed that by her not doing that, that she was just solidifying the thought that she really didn't care about me, that I was an inconvenience to her and her life, and that I absolutely was a mistake that she would rather forget. I was on a rampage when I turned eighteen, I was going to find her and that under no circumstances was she going to deny me *my* rights. My right to know; my right to understand; my right to answers; my right to have her face me and see the person that gave me away; my right to show her that it was her loss since she decided to throw me away like an old dirty sock. It was my right to know what happened that made her make that decision, my right to know who my father was, and above all, my right to know **_who I was_**. It was because of the choices that were made for me, for my life, for my existence, that I didn't know who I was, really. Where I came from, who I took after, who I looked like, who I acted like were empty holes that I desperately wanted to fill. The only way I could ever explain it to anyone that ever asked me how I felt about being adopted and not knowing who my family was or where I came from, was with a simple answer:

"I'm me, but I'm not."

I came to the realization that yes, these answers are absolutely 100% owed to me, but the reality was that I would never get those answers; I would not be allowed the right to those answers. Because of her choices that I had no say and no rights in, essentially my thoughts, feelings, and emotions were all her fault; I needed to place blame. Someone needed to be responsible for it, and take responsibility for it because in my mind, these were out of my control. Growing up trying to understand all this in our heads, and make sense of it can be extremely overwhelming. This is especially when you think no one can possibly understand what you're thinking or feeling.

This is why communication with your family is so important. Sometimes just talking about feelings, asking questions out loud to each other or brainstorming can be a huge relief mentally and emotionally. Just feeling heard at the very least, even if if not completely understood, can make you feel like the weight of the world has been lifted from you. However, sometimes this can cause even more questions to pop up. One question unanswered can lead to five more you never thought of.

2. 1000 QUESTIONS

It is absolutely 100% normal to have hundreds of thousands of questions. There are so many questions that go unanswered because sometimes there is little to no information given to the adoption agency or to the adopted parents when you're born.

There are a few lucky ones that get tons of information and then there are the unlucky ones that get barely anything.

With all of the adoptees that I have spoken with, I have found that no matter how much or how little information that the adoptee gets, there is always a myriad of questions that will usually be present.

Generally, the questions and daydreams that happen are usually in the younger years up to the early 20's. The usual questions seem to always start with:

"Who am I?"
"Who do I look like?"
"Who am I most like?"
"Am I anything like my mom?"
"Am I anything like my dad?"

There are always a lot of questions, and every one of them are completely understandable, and legitimate. There is not one single question you have that could ever be considered silly, stupid, or unrealistic. They're your questions, sprung from your own mind, from your own thoughts and every single one of them is real.

It's very hard to know who you are when you don't know where you came from. You can't help but make up scenarios in your mind of who you might really be, where you might really be from, and how your life may have gone, or played out differently if you hadn't been adopted.

For me, I used to make up all kinds of typical little girl scenarios in my imagination where I was really a princess. There was some huge sordid affair and my mother was in love with someone who wasn't a prince, and she became pregnant with me and was forced to give me up for adoption in secret so that no one would know about her indiscretion, and the kingdom would be none the wiser.

In my imagination, I truly believed at one point that this scenario was real, and that one day my real mother would come for me and I would live a life of freedom, luxury, jewels and castles. I would get to wear beautiful ball gowns and tiaras, get to dance at lavish balls, only to be courted by handsome princes. I think pretty well every little girl on the planet has imagined this scenario more than once in their lives growing up, not just adopted ones!

That this type of fantasy is common among adoptees can be seen in countless news stories about people who go to the media or even launch court battles demanding DNA testing, certain that they're the long-lost illegitimate child of a celebrity, or European nobility. While their heartfelt beliefs far more often than not turn out to be mistakes, the fact that so many adoptees will go to such lengths to confirm their stories shows just how deeply the *need to know* runs through the human soul.

Other times, I imagined that I would have lived in extreme poverty and despair. I would spend my childhood living from house to house, sometimes out of our old car. Living in shelters and sometimes under the stars. I liked to imagine that I was rescued by my adopted parents, and that my life would have been horribly poor and destitute.

I often wondered all the usual questions that adoptees all have. I often wondered who I looked more like, who I acted more like, and if my mother liked the same things I did. I often wondered if we had the same taste in food, clothes and colours.

The biggest question I always had, was if she

thought about me. I wondered if she regretted giving me up. I wondered if she wished she had kept me. I wondered if she had any other children after me, or before me. I wondered if she ever told anyone about me or if I was a big secret that no one ever knew about. I wondered if my father knew about me. I wondered if she ever told him about me. I wondered if he decided with her to give me up, or if he forced her to. I wondered if I looked or acted like him.

There are so many questions that go through your head that sometimes you will think that your head will explode. Just when you think you can't possibly have any more questions, another one you never thought of before will pop up out of nowhere. This usually starts the endless circle of questions all over again, seemingly never-ending. This may only last a few days or weeks, however sometimes it lasts for years. There is never any question that you could have that another adoptee hasn't already had. I must stress again that there is never a silly or stupid question, that every single question you have is completely understandable, and valid to each person. Although most adoptees have the same thought processes, there are no right or wrong ways to think or feel.

Sometimes, the only questions that you want answered are medical questions. Maybe you're having health issues and you need to know where they come from, or if they're from only one side of the family, or both. Are any of these health issues hereditary or are they only from yourself? Are there any other health issues that run in the family that you need to know about? Is there anything that runs in the family that you need to be aware of that may be a deadly disease? Doctors will often ask these questions of their patients and it can be difficult or even embarrassing to have to admit that you don't know the answers.

No matter what the questions, or how many there are, the one thing that you can rest assured of, is that it's completely normal to have endless amounts of questions.

You're in the dark about anything to do with who you are, where you come from, and what your background is. And, you aren't the only one that asks what seems like a billion questions. I haven't spoken to one adoptee yet that hasn't had at the very least, a handful of questions.

The hardest part about being the adoptee is that you don't have the answers. Your adoptive parents don't have the answers. The old saying that "ignorance is bliss" absolutely does _not_ apply in this situation. Ignorance is not bliss, on the contrary, it's sheer agony. The not knowing really is the worst part of any of it. You don't know how to think, act, walk, talk, eat, breathe, dress etc… It's horrible. You always question if you're doing it right, or wrong, or like someone else, or like yourself. But, that's the problem; you don't know if you _are_ being yourself!

The other hard part about this is that you don't know _who_ has the answers, or if they even have any answers at all. You don't know if you can talk to your adopted parents about it because you don't know if they will understand why you are asking so many questions. You aren't sure if they will understand the way you feel, especially since you don't think anyone understands how you feel. Then there's also the possibility that your birth parents don't want to talk to you and give you the answers you have the right to know, that you *need* to know.

Thus, starting the vicious circle I spoke about earlier. You start questioning yourself, and it starts all over again.

The one thing that I started doing when I was younger, was writing down all my questions in a journal. I started including what my feelings were and why. I found that it really helped me try to sort out what I was feeling. Sometimes I could get some answers, and sometimes, I couldn't.

This is where I emphasize how important it is to communicate. Communicate with your adoptive parents.

And, adoptive parents, you have to communicate with your adopted child, I can not stress this enough. It is your responsibility to make sure that you communicate as much as you possibly can in the most understanding way that you can. Don't forget, this child was given no say, and no choice in their lives. They have been thrown into a situation that was chosen for them, that you chose for them. You won't be able to answer all (or sometimes any) questions that your adoptive child may have, but, you will be able to listen and give empathy and support when your child needs it most.

3. COMMUNICATION IS KEY

Communication is paramount between adoptive parents and their adopted children. There are going to be so many questions and emotions for both of you that it may be hard to shuffle through it all if you try to address them all at once.

I have one major rule that must be followed to the letter if there is to be harmony between adoptive parents and adoptees:

NEVER LIE

That's it. It's that simple. Never ever lie.

Always tell the truth as soon as you can and as early as you can. If you lie, or cover it up, or simply avoid it entirely and never tell the truth about it, I can promise you this: It **_WILL_** come back to haunt you.

Eventually, some way, somehow, the truth WILL come out, and your child WILL resent you, or even hate you for lying to them. Any relationship that you have, any trust you have, any bonds you have, will be destroyed. You will never get it back. Ever.

A lie by omission is still a lie.

It's always best to have this talk as early as possible. Before school age if the child is mentally and emotionally capable of it. Some children are, and some aren't. You, as the parent will know when their communication skills are strong enough to handle the conversation.

I can not stress enough the importance of honesty. Honesty is the biggest key to making sure that your child can understand and process what you are going to talk about. If they don't feel that they can trust you, this conversation is going to be much harder on both of you.

If they can't trust you, then it won't matter how much you tell them you love them and want them, they will not believe it. Children are more perceptive and have a better understanding than many adults and parents give them credit for. If they feel that they can trust you, the conversation will go smoothly and will help keep the child's mental and emotional state in tact, as well as create an unbreakable bond that will last a lifetime. This is a sacred bond that you must cherish and nurture. This is the most critical stage of your relationship with your adopted child, and their relationship with you.

I was told from a very young age, before school age,

that I was someone special, someone a little different from everyone else, but in one of the best ways possible. I will share my story a little later, however, I'm beyond grateful that I was told so young, and the way my parents chose to do it was absolutely perfect. Everyone that I have spoken with that has heard the story, have all agreed that it was a very smooth way of getting the conversation started, and keeping it going, while never breaking the bond of trust, but by strengthening it.

Adopted parents may feel that they are inadequate to answer the questions that will come up, and as children, they will expect that the parents will have all the answers, because no matter what, adopted or not, children put parents up on a pedestal with expectations of invincibility, power and unlimited knowledge.

For parents, this may be difficult for you, but you need to remember patience and understanding, especially at this time. Although I already pointed out earlier that children are much more understanding and perceptive than we give them credit for, there will be for some, possible difficulty in their full digestion of this situation. They may not fully grasp the concept of adoption, or understand that they are not your biological child, so these issues need to be touched on very lightly and at age appropriate times, in language that they can understand, and process. Again, you will know the best way to approach this with them and use terms that you know they will be able to grasp. There is no one way to do this, and no one specific way that works better than another.

We always hope our children can understand what we are telling them and why. We always hope that we are explaining it in a way they can understand it. Many children can have this conversation as young as 3 or 4. For others, it's more appropriate to do it around ages 5 or 6. Only you as the parent will know when the time is just right to start the conversation.

Some parents tend to sometimes forget that children have a harder time understanding, dissecting, analyzing, and digesting information that is given to them. They don't have the knowledge or wisdom that parents have because they haven't been subjected to the world at large, in all its true ugliness and beauty. They don't have a functioning understanding of relationships, sex, or even marriage.

They pick up on keywords, phrases, and statements that they think they understand, and that is what will stick in their heads, so extra explanations may be needed, sometimes extensive and exhausting extra explanations. But, you need to remember that a child may be asking the same question over and over because they either don't understand it, or they are simply trying to process and digest it in a manner that they can understand.

First and foremost, before you start ANY conversation

with your child, you need to make sure that they understand 100% clearly that you unconditionally love them no matter what. That they are the most special and prized thing in your life. You can't start into the adoption conversation until they really know and understand this.

You also must be sure that there is no question in your mind about their understanding, you should feel certain that they do indeed understand this. This will make the next round of information easier to process because they know and understand that they ARE loved and wanted. I find that more times than not, it's the realization that the mother gave them away is the most detrimental and crushing information they will ever hear.

It's also extremely important that whether or not you know the reasons that the child was put up for adoption, that you never, and I can't stress enough, **_NEVER_** bash the birth parent, or say anything negative about them, or why they had to choose to give up their child. This will not only put them in a bad light, but you as well. Rather, it's best to explain to them that there are sometimes certain things that can happen in someone's life that can make them have to make choices that may not be best for them, but best for the person it most directly affects.

Or, you can simply tell them that because their mother didn't think she could provide a good enough life for them because of her own reasons, that she loved the child so much that she wanted to do what she felt was best for them to grow up in a wonderfully happy life with people that were better equipped to give a good happy healthy life… of course, you'd put it in the wording best suited to your child. These are only suggestions to start the conversation, a guide to help you figure out how best to approach it. You, as a parent may find a completely different way to go about it that may be just as effective, if not better. Every person is different on how they start this important conversation, just as much as every person is different on how they receive or perceive it.

As long as you can explain the birth mother's possible choices in a non-biased way, the child will feel that the birth mother is not the enemy, or someone to be disliked, or hated, but someone that wanted to do something that was best for them and give them a good life with good people that can care for him or her in the best way possible. Also, explain to them that you are sure that this decision was very hard for the mother to make and positive that it wasn't made lightly. Make sure that they understand that being able to give away something you love very dearly is not an easy thing to do.

You could possibly give them an example of one of their own toys or pets that they love with all their hearts... see if they can understand how hard it would be to give one of them away to someone that they don't know because you think they would have a better life with them… like maybe a favourite dog or cat … or a favourite stuffed toy… maybe someone else would give them a better life if they had a bigger house, or bigger yard to run in, and afford to feed it steak every day, or a nicer bedroom for they toy. Whatever example helps them understand.

Children already have a basic understanding that the mother is the one that carries the baby in their tummy, so when the child hears that the person that is supposed to be their mommy didn't want to keep them, it puts immediate doubts of self worth into their heads. They immediately feel that they were unwanted and not important or loved enough to be kept by *someone*.

This will, unfortunately, create trust issues to some degree, between you and your child. It may also lead to trust issues with other people that surround them as they grow up like friends, or, as they grow older, girlfriends and boyfriends… possibly even husbands or wives. This is why it is so important, and I can't stress enough, monumentally important, to communicate, and be as open and honest as you can. There is a serious trust bond between you and the child that you have to ensure you don't sever. This will cause more heartache for all of you in the long run, as well as mental and emotional issues that may never be able to be resolved.

The trust and self esteem issues will happen to some degree no matter how much you tell them that YOU love them and want them and are the most important thing in your life. It's inevitable.

Even if they don't act like it, or tell you that they are fine with it and understand it, they will *still* think about it, and it *will* play on their mind. While there's no way around that, make sure to keep the communication lines open and the bond of trust will stay strong.

This is why starting off with positivity is so important.

So that when they hear the "bad news", it might make it easier for them to digest and process.

Over time, they may be able to get a more firm understanding of what the adoption process is, and be able to form a better bond with you as parents once there is a solid belief that there is true, unconditional love from you as parents. That you really do mean it when you say you love them. Children learn just as much from words as they do actions. If you say that you love them, then act like it and treat them, as well as others like them... with kindness, caring and compassion.

There is nothing more important in this world than a strong bond between parents and their children, especially mother and child, whether it's a biological or not.

There are going to be so many questions that you may or may not be able to answer. The ones that you can, answer as honestly as possible. The ones that you can't, make sure you are honest about that too, and explain that you don't have the answer. The child will appreciate your honesty and trust you *more* for it.

Don't forget, you've just told them more or less that everything they have ever thought or known is not what it seems, and not what they believe to be the truth. So this conversation needs to be handled in a very delicate manner, no matter how you decide to do it.

There may, or may not, depending on how the conversation goes, be abandonment issues that arise that will need to be addressed. Those can be a very touchy issue and need to be dealt with in a very delicate manner so as not to further injure their feelings.

Feelings of abandonment are all too often the dominant and most powerful feeling of all, as well as being the most damaging, with the strongest long term effects. Sometimes they present themselves in very obvious ways, sometimes they're more subtle, or even subconscious. But those feelings are there. To some degree, they're there; they always will be.

4. WHAT DO I DO IF THE CONVERSATION DOESN'T GO WELL?

In the event that the child doesn't take the news well, there are a few options that you can consider. Firstly, you could ask the child if they want to continue the conversation and figure it out together, or if they would like to talk about it later. Make it their choice. After all, this is about them and their life. This information may turn their whole life upside down in their little heads. Everything that they thought and knew is all different now.

This is where things will sometimes get very sticky and difficult. If they decide that they don't want to talk about it, and refuse to hear about it, then you have little choice but to respect that decision, and not discuss it further until they come to you and want to talk about it.

Just let them know that you understand how they are feeling and that you will be there at any time when and if they are ready to talk. After some time goes by, they will eventually come around and want to talk to you. Make sure that you make yourself available to them when this time comes, as it may be the only opportunity you get. If you consistently divert the conversation, or don't make time for them when they need it, they may never try to talk to you about it again as they now have the impression that it's too much trouble or that you don't want to discuss it.

This may lead to larger problems later on, with many unresolved issues, feelings and questions they may have. They may start to feel a deeper resentment towards not only their birth parents, but to you as the adoptive parents, as well as towards themselves. They may, over time, start to blame you and them for things that have gone wrong in their life, even if it is because of their own poor choices.

This can also lead to larger abandonment issues within them.

Abandonment issues can take on many forms. They can range from feelings of low self esteem, to self loathing, right up to a sudden onset of obsessive compulsions.

There could be anger issues as well as feelings of instability and resentment. They may misdirect their resentment towards their birth parents (more specifically the mother, as I already mentioned) for possibly putting them in a position in their life that they don't want to be in, or believe that they shouldn't be in. They can resent their adoptive parents as well, believing that you are somehow responsible for choosing a worse path in life for them that they may have had, had you not adopted them in the first place.

This could, in turn, cause the anger issues. They could start lashing out because of how they are feeling. The constant questions swirling around in their heads of "who am I?" "where do I come from?" "is there anyone else in my family that is like this?" It's the not knowing, the uncertainty, the confusion, and, above all, being scared. An old saying that comes to mind is the one about fearing the unknown and this is very true here as well. When people are afraid, they often get angry and then they lash out. They may not mean to, but since they don't have the right tools to help them cope with their feelings and emotions, or the right tools to learn how to understand them they can't help themselves.

Again, this falls true to the title of my book: "I'm Me But I'm Not." And that can be very confusing.

The feelings of low self esteem and self loathing can be alleviated with constant confirmations to the child of love, affection, and above all, importance. This isn't just achieved by monetary things, and many people often make that mistake. This is done with a lot of patience, kindness, gentleness, and positive reinforcement both verbally and physically.

It's amazing how you can change someone's outlook on something with a few simple words like "have I told you today how much I love you and how grateful I am for you?" while giving them a hug. This is why I mentioned before how it's important to not just say the words, but act like it as well. There's an old saying about actions speaking louder than words… but if you combine both words and actions, then it's not just loud, it's more like a scream!

Above all, be patient. They're trying to figure it all out, just like you are. The difference is, you as the parent, and as an adult, have a clearer understanding of who you are, where you came from, the path you're on, and answers to any or all of your questions. They don't.

They will be looking to you to provide these answers, and chances are, most of their questions you won't have the answers to. But, you have to figure out an answer that will work best for both of you, as honestly as possible.

Avoid responding with your own worries and concerns, this is especially true with younger children. Avoid asking questions like "Why do you want to know?" or "Why? Are you unhappy with us? Or our family?" Your child's curiosity is healthy and natural. That last thing you want to do is make them feel like they are upsetting you. This can scare the child into thinking they are hurting you or making you unhappy, and all children want nothing more than to please their parents. They may close up on you thinking it's only upsetting you, and that it will please you to hear only what they know will make you happy and not sad. This isn't healthy communication.

5. WHAT HAPPENS IF THE CONVERSATION GOES WELL?

AWESOME!!!

It's absolutely fantastic if the conversation goes well! If they are open to it, and responsive to it, then that is absolutely the best possible outcome any adoptive parent can ask for!

If you start off the conversation and it's well received, then keep going in a positive manner in order to keep the conversation going!

This is where it gets really interesting. You are going

to get barraged with a ton of questions, many of them you may not be able to answer, and that's still ok! Just continue to answer the best that you can, and of course, be honest.

Remember to let them know that you are always available to talk about it more and answer their questions as best as you can. Still, stay on track with not bashing the birth parents. Don't make them out to be the bad guy in hopes that it will make you look better to the child because it won't. Stay true and honest no matter what.

Remember, they are probably going to also be scared to ask questions, for fear that they might hear an answer they don't want to know, or that they might upset you by asking something. Never let them think that any question they have is bad, or a wrong one, or that their questions will upset you. Because, honestly and truly, it *shouldn't*. It's natural that some questions may be difficult for you to answer, or to hear, but, as their parent, they need to unequivocally know without a shadow of a doubt, that they can, talk to you, be open with you, be honest with you and above all - *TRUST YOU.*

In the event that you are the adoptee, and you don't have a good relationship with your adoptive parents, then you can find a good support group, maybe some very close friends, a sibling, members of your church, or even people in adoption groups online, or in person. There are so many more places for support and help these days than there ever was in the past. So, if you don't have the support, or the blessing from your adoptive family to go on your search, then see what options are available to you in your area. The adoption agency that you get your information from may be able to help you with support groups in your area. It never hurts to ask.

6. THEY WANT TO FIND THEIR BIRTH PARENTS – NOW WHAT?

This can be a really tough conversation. Not just for the child, but for the parents too.

There is really nothing that can be done until the required age is met for the laws according to wherever it is that you live. Each province or state has its own laws regarding this, and what the minimum age is to be able to get the first step of information, which is the non-identifying information.

The non-identifying information is generally, as a rule, any and all information collected by the adoption agency prior to, or at the time of the birth. It's provided by any and all birth relatives that are included in the adoption process.

Normally, it gives information like time and date of birth, hospital name or location, name given at birth, and any information given about family history, or family medical history. Sometimes it will tell you the kind of occupation the birth parents or family members had, and sometimes even the age of the birth mother at the time that the birth occurred.

Some adoptees are very lucky and get a wealth of information provided by the birth mother, and sometimes a grandparent or aunt as well.

It never gives out any identifying information such as parents names, relatives names or anything like that. That's why it's called non-identifying.

Sometimes, there is little to no information given by the birth mother or the family, and that is a shame for the adoptees that are looking for information or answers.

Where I live, at the age of 18 the adoptee can apply to the agency the adoption took place for this information. This can be a very long wait list from months, to even years, just for this information.

I always recommend that at the time that you finally do get the non-identifying information, to immediately apply for the identifying information, whether you want to know it or not. The reason for this, is because the wait list for that information can be many many years before you get it. Once they have it ready, they will contact you and let you know it's ready to be picked up in person. At that time, you can decide if you want it or not since it's left there in your file until you are ready to collect it. It's better to have it sitting there waiting for you when you're ready for it, than to really want it and not be able to get it.

There is definitely a crazy myriad of feelings and emotions that will go into this conversation. On both the adoptive parents' side as well as the adoptee's.

The biggest fear on both sides, is that the other one will feel a sense of betrayal towards the other.

Sometimes, the adoptive parents may feel betrayed that the child wants to find out who their birth parents are. They may feel insecure about a meeting taking place because there's always the "what if" factor. This is a really scary process for everyone involved. Adoptive parents may have very serious feelings towards this topic, and not in a good way. Just as the child may have severe anxiety about this, so can the adoptive parents. Just like with adoptees, we always explain that their thoughts and feelings about these issues are completely valid and understandable, and that all adoptees go through them in one way or another; adoptive parents have the same anxieties, just on the other side of it. Too many times, the focus is put on the adoptee, and how they feel about it all, so we need to make sure that the adoptive parents are addressed on these issues as well. Adoptive parents go through just as much mentally and emotionally as the adoptees do, but just on the other side of the fence. So, as an adoptive parent, you're absolutely not alone in this. All adoptive parents go through the same things, feelings, emotions, anxieties, and questions.

So we need to make sure that we address this side of it so that the adoptive parents can also feel a sense of understanding and validity here as well.

Some thoughts or questions an adoptive parent might have include, but certainly aren't limited to:

What if they are really good people that my son or daughter really gets along with and likes better?

What if they have more money than us?

What if they have a bigger house?

What if they are more fun?

What if they can provide better than we can?

What if they decide they want their child back?

What if my child wants to go live with them?

These kinds of thoughts can lead to feelings of depression and anger. Sometimes, those questions can turn into scenarios that play out over and over again in your head, which cause you to over analyze the situation, as well as all the possible outcomes. You may get a certain scenario in your head of how something might play out, like the adoptee meeting their birth parent(s) and realizing that some of those "what if" questions could come true.

Maybe they meet and they really do get along, and start forming a relationship. There is a chance that there will be feelings of betrayal by the adoptive parents, as well as anger caused by the feelings of betrayal.

This may create strong feelings of inadequacy in the adoptive parents while in reality nothing could be further from the truth. This is no different than if your best friend suddenly makes another friend! You're no less important to them, they've just found someone else to enjoy the company of as well.

You have to be prepared for this. As an adoptive parent, it can be very difficult to understand the feelings and emotions that your adopted child will go through, but you need to be as understanding as possible and remember not to take anything they may say or do personally. This is not about you, it is about them, their search to find themselves, to figure out who they really are, where they came from, and hopefully have all their questions answered.

You may find that you start questioning yourself and getting angry. Many adoptive parents go through this, it's completely understandable. Some even will voice these feelings to their adopted child very freely, without thinking how much the things they say may affect how the adoptee already feels, and may compound the already crazy swirling emotional typhoon they are already experiencing. This can also lead to feelings of animosity between not just yourself and your adoptee, but between yourself and the birth family and, by extension, the adoptee and their birth family.

If you're quick to voice your negative feelings, statements often come out in the form of:

Why are you doing this to us?

Haven't we been good enough parents to you?

After everything we've done for you, you want to find them?

And so on. Of course, you don't mean for them to come out in a negative or hurtful way, but they do.

You're scared for both yourself and your child. You don't want to lose them, or even feel like you've already lost them and you certainly don't want them to get hurt if the outcome is not what they hoped for. You don't want to get hurt either.

When an adoptee makes the decision and announces that they want to find their birth family, or that they are meeting with them, it can be devastating for some adoptive parents. There are many processes and emotions that happen when this announcement happens.

I equivocate these emotions similar to receiving bad health news, or about the untimely death of a loved one.

I'll explain how it may go:

- Shock / Denial

For some adoptive parents, the announcement can come as a shock, especially if there has been no real prior communication about the issue. This can also lead to denial that "they really don't mean that" which is another reason why communicating about it is so crucial.

- Anger

You can become angry. Angry with the questions I spoke about earlier of wanting to know "why this is being done to you". Fear can lead to anger, fear is also another form of anger. Again, this can lead to lashing out about the issue verbally, emotionally, and sometimes, sadly, physically.

- Bargaining

You may find yourself trying to convince them not to search. Trying to find alternate ways to appease them. Sometimes it's with money by offering extravagant gifts or trips for example. You may find yourself trying to convince them other routes would be better, counseling perhaps or maybe trying to plan other things with the adoptive family instead.

- Depression

The pronouncement of the decision to search can lead to a very deep feeling of despair and loss in adoptive parents. This despair can only be compared to that of the loss of a loved one and can easily lead to depression. Even though there is no actual loss, it can still feel that way. It can feel as if you are losing the adoptive child, even when you really aren't. They are just looking to explore who they are and where they came from. All they know is that they feel different and they are different... they just aren't sure why. This is part of being "I'm me but I'm not." You know who you are, and why, but at the same time, you don't. This is the endless mental and emotional struggle of an adoptee that they will eventually need closure to, one way or another.

And, lastly,

- Acceptance

This sometimes doesn't ever happen. There are some adoptive parents that will absolutely refuse to accept that it is going to happen, is happening, or already happened. There are some that will eventually, over time, resign themselves to the realization that it is inevitable and will happen whether they like it or not. Sometimes, the adoptive parent will come around, and even join in to having a friendly relationship with the birth parent or family member.

On the other hand, there are some adoptive parents that are extremely open to the idea of their child finding their birth family. Some will not only accept and understand it, but even participate and actively help in the search. These are the ones that generally have very open communication with their child about adoption and that they are adopted.

The bottom line is, as an adoptive parent, you need to at least try to understand how the adoptee is feeling. This is a very difficult time for them where they are trying to figure out so many things, and having to deal with negative reaction from the parents that they do know and love will only compound their already existing apprehensions about the whole thing.

Again, I stress - open and honest communication. That the only way to have any attempt at understanding each other.

7. I WANT TO FIND MY BIRTH PARENTS – NOW WHAT?

Well, you just finished the last chapter, so we know potentially how the adoptive parents may, or may not feel and/or react.

But, now, it's time to talk about how you, the adoptee, might feel and/or react. And, although it's pretty much the same, it's actually quite different. And only another adoptee really understands that.

It's completely normal to have the desire to want to find your "real parents" as adoptees often refer to them. This falls under the same desire to want all your questions answered. You'd love to know why you were given up, what it was like to make that choice, who they are, who do you look like, who do you act like, what kind of life you may have had if you hadn't been placed for adoption.

These are the reasons that you feel like yourself, but you don't. Those are the reasons I used to always ask the same questions myself, and why I used to always say "I'm me, but I'm not." I must have driven my parents nuts with the endless string of questions I constantly asked.

I was very lucky. We had an amazing open communication about the whole adoption issue. When I asked them what they thought of me wanting to find my "real mom", they completely understood and proceeded to help me find out just how to go about doing that. They actually voiced numerous times that they would love to meet her and firstly, thank her for giving them their daughter, and secondly, just out of curiosity to see how much her and I were alike.

Starting this process can be very scary. You start playing out the endless possibilities in your head about how it might play out, and how you hope it will play out.

I can't express enough about communicating with your adoptive parents about this. You may feel that you are somehow betraying them, betraying their trust, and their love. This is also completely normal. If you are one of the lucky ones to have a great relationship and open communication with them, and you've had the conversation, if they've given you the "go-ahead" to search, then do it. If they tell you that they understand and they want you to go ahead and search, then you really shouldn't worry! They understand. Really, they do.

The first thing you need to do (once you are the legal

age to do this in the area in which you live) is find out where the adoption took place, and contact them. They will guide you through the process of what you need to apply for, in what order, and how to do it.

They are usually very backed up with cases, so don't expect results immediately. Sometimes just getting the first step of information (the non-identifying) can take many many years. The agency can usually give you a rough idea of the time frame you are looking at to receive any information at all. Depending on where you're adopted out of, the wait for this can be a few months, up to a couple of years.

I already mentioned this before, but I will mention it again because it is so important. I always recommend that at the time that you finally do get the non-identifying information, to immediately apply for the identifying information. Whether you want to know it or not. The reason for this, is because the wait list for that information can be many many years before you get it. Once they have it ready, they will contact you and let you know it's ready to be picked up in person. At that time, you can decide if you want it or not. It's left there in your file until you are ready to collect it. It's better to have it sitting there waiting for you when you're ready for it, than to really want it and not be able to get it.

If you are one of the very lucky people, and very FEW people that get a LOT of information, as I was lucky enough to get, you can sometimes have enough to go on where you would want to hire a private investigator yourself and maybe they can help point you in the right direction to who they may be. I don't usually recommend going this route and I will tell you why.

Sometimes, unfortunately, the birth parents don't want to be found. They just want to forget it ever happened. Sometimes they have decided that they have moved on with their lives and that you are in their past and want to keep the past in the past.

This can be very hard to hear, and you'll have to deal with the feeling of rejection all over again. You may think that it won't affect you. But it will. It always does, in one way or another, it does. You come to realize that they rejected you at birth, and are now rejecting you again. You may also experience the feelings of anger that would go along with the rejection. This is where you have to be very careful with both your head and heart. There are so many ways this can affect you mentally and emotionally.

This can also lead to the same stages as the 5 stages of grief... as I explained in the previous chapter... but in a slightly different way.

I ALWAYS recommend that you do NOT go in search of your birth family on your own. Always, I repeat, **always** have someone else do it for you on your behalf. If the meeting doesn't go in a positive way, it can be very destructive not only to their lives, but yours - maybe they didn't tell anyone that they had a child that they gave up, maybe it was all done in secret, maybe their lives have gone in a completely different direction than they thought it would and they don't ever want to look into the past. Maybe they have husbands, wives and children now that will not understand or be prepared for such a huge shift in their world.

Maybe, if it were done in a discreet manner, if they *did* want to have communication with you and were allowed to prepare themselves and their families better before an abrupt and drastic announcement, then the outcome would be more positive and welcomed. But, if you just barge into their world announcing your presence unprepared, it may go horribly wrong, when it may have gone better if planned out properly.

Plus, if it IS a negative response, you do not want to be the bearer of that bad news directly. You need to have someone that is as unattached emotionally as possible to be able to break the news to you in a softer way than it may be received if you were to hear it to your face. The rejection cushioning may be easier to handle.

This is why any and all communications, interactions and correspondence should always be done by someone you trust who is somewhat unattached to the issue. A close friend, an aunt, a sibling, a member of your church, but absolutely someone you implicitly trust.

I'll explain how a direct or indirect rejection may play out emotionally in the 5 stages:

- Shock / Denial

For some adoptees, this can come as a shock, especially if you set your hopes far too high, and your expectations too high. I'm not saying that you shouldn't have hopes, dreams and expectations, but what I am saying is that you need to keep them realistic at all times. If you are realistic about it, then you will also realize that the potential for a meeting may, or may not, ever be there. This is also where having open communication with your family, or your support team can be extremely beneficial. You can discuss what realistic possibilities there are with them and not trick yourself into thinking things will go a certain way, when in fact, they just may not.

- Anger

You can become angry. Angry with the questions I spoke about earlier of wanting to know "why this is being done to you". As I pointed out before, fear can lead to anger and is even another form of anger. Again, this can lead to lashing out about the issue verbally, emotionally, and sometimes, sadly, physically. Anger is one of the harder emotions to dissect. You may start feeling angry with them and feeling like they owe you an answer, any answer. And you're right, you should be given an answer to something. It's not fair, or right that you aren't given the opportunity of knowing all the why's. But, unfortunately, sometimes, with anything in life, we don't always get the answer to the why. This is where you really need to have open communication with your support group, or your adoptive family, to help you work through this horrible way of feeling.

• Bargaining

You may find yourself trying to convince them that they need to see you, meet you or talk to you. You may find yourself begging for communication, this can also lead to possibly starting to stalk them, showing up where they shop, go to school, their workplace etc. which can only lead to a very bad situation as I don't think I need to explain. Even if you don't see yourself as a stalker, that may not be how your birth family perceives it. These situations can be very easy to get into, but very hard to get out of. This is one of the main reasons I always suggest to never, ever be the one to initiate any contact. Always have someone you trust do it for you as it does tend to make any negative reaction a little easier to digest.

- Depression

Another negative emotion that may raise its head from being rejected would be depression. Depression of this kind can be very destructive to an adoptee's already fragile ego and emotions. Again, it would be a very deep feeling of despair and loss that can only be compared to that of the loss of a loved one or the loss of a parent. Even though there is no actual loss, it can still feel that way. It can feel as if you are losing a critical part of your life when you really aren't. I used to always tell people that it wouldn't happen to me because you can't miss what you never had. This is far from the truth. You can miss what you dreamed of having. What you hoped of having. This is another time that your support circle as well as the open communication with your adoptive parents is crucial. They will help you through what can potentially be a very dark time emotionally, and show you the love and support that you desperately will need at this time.

And, lastly,

- Acceptance

This sometimes doesn't ever happen. There are some adoptees that will absolutely refuse to accept that their birth family doesn't want to have a relationship with them. This is much harder to digest for some people than others, and can lead to serious repercussions in everyone's lives. However, there are some that will eventually, over time, resign themselves to the realization that it is not going to happen whether they like it or not. Sometimes, they just learn to cope with the feelings and emotions of it through communication, and their support circles. Over time, most adoptees do learn to deal with it, and adjust to it. I find the older we get, the better we learn to deal and cope with how it all plays out. Again, support circles are monumentally important to learning how to mentally and emotionally survive.

More often than not, when you find yourself searching in an aggressive manner, it's because you think you're missing something. You have this feeling like there's something else out there, that "the grass might be greener on the other side of the fence". You have to approach this in a structured, paced, and realistic manner. We all know that saying of "jumping in with both feet and eyes closed". Make sure that you know what you are searching for, why, and most importantly, what you realistically hope to find. This is the best way to protect your mental and emotional health.

8. QUESTIONS MOST ADOPTEES GET ASKED

1. My favourite question - How does it feel to be adopted?

Easy. I'm me, but I'm not.

2. Are you really adopted?

Yes, of course I am. What an odd question. It's beyond me why anyone would want to lie about being adopted, unless they're ashamed of their current family, maybe? It's entirely possible. But, yes, we hear that question a lot.

3. Do you know your real parents?

I always answer this question with "Yes, I know my real parents. They are the ones that raised me. If you mean the people that created me or gave birth to me, then no, I don't know who they are."

4. Are you going to look for them?

I don't know why everyone is always so eager to ask this question right after I give them the answer to the question asking if I know who they are. To me, and maybe only to me, that answer is pretty obvious that my "real parents" aren't really a concern in my daily life. Maybe I should think of a better answer to that last question rather than a sarcastic one and I may get asked this question less.

5. Have you always known you were adopted?

Well, no, my parents told me I was. This isn't something you just know. It has to be told to you. Sure, sometimes you think something is "off" or that you're somehow "different" if you aren't told right away or at a young age, but yes, ultimately someone has to tell you this information.

6. Why did your parents adopt you?

Well, usually this is a pretty simple guess for most people, but, for some reason, they not only want to know why I was adopted, they want to know which one of my parents couldn't have children. This is apparently important knowledge for a large number of people.

7. So why did your mom give you up?

Again, most people think that adoptees miraculously

have the answers to these questions. Unless you have already met your birth mother, or birth family, chances are you don't know. And, usually I find that again, people ask this after they have already asked if I know who she is or if we've met. If the answer to the first two questions is no, then chances are the answer to this one will be "I don't know."

8. OMG! What if you were to find out that you actually slept with or married one of your siblings!? EW!

sigh Yes, this is asked more than you can ever imagine.

9. Is your name your real name or is it the one your mom gave you?

Again, I go straight for the sarcasm on this one. I always say "Yes, it's my real name. If my name was Mickey Mouse then I'm sure it would be a fake. If you're asking if my name is the name I was given at birth by my birth mother, then, no. This is the name my parents chose for me when they adopted me."

10. Do you want to meet your birth parents?

Sure, one day maybe. I'm not on a mega-mission to find them, but I wouldn't say no if they found me first.

I'm sure there's many more questions that adoptees get asked, so I chose a few that I know are asked to almost every single adoptee I have ever talked to. Some are ridiculous questions, and some are downright rude ones. It's all in the way you handle them, the way you answer them that matters. If you don't want to answer anyone, then just tell them flat out that you don't want to talk about it. Don't be shy, they certainly aren't. Don't ever feel that you have to answer any questions you don't want to.

9. QUESTIONS MOST ADOPTIVE PARENTS GET ASKED

1. Why did you adopt? Couldn't you have children?

First off, it's the rudest, most invasive and inappropriate question I have ever heard anyone ask. And, yes, people do ask. Flat out, with no filter, no regard for the person's feelings. Don't get angry if you're asked this question. Every single adoptive parent on Earth gets asked this. So, be prepared to answer. If you're going to announce that you're adopting, or that you have just adopted, you're opening the door to some of the most bizarre, ignorant, invasive, hurtful, and flat out rude questions you could imagine. Be prepared for them by having your own personal "standard responses" in your head.

2. Where did you get him/her?

Because I generally go to the sarcasm when I get asked ridiculous questions, I would answer this in a passive-aggressive way by saying something like "Oh, her? She was a K-Mart blue light special. We lost the receipt and can't take her back now, so we have to keep her." But that's just me. How you answer is entirely up to you.

3. Don't you wish you could have had your own children?

Well of course ANY parent would want that!

4. What if they turn out bad? Can you take them back?

It's not a car with faulty wiring, or an item with a manufacturer's defect for goodness sakes! You can't just take it back and ask for a new and improved model!

5. Why would you have a baby shower? You're not pregnant.

Well, that's like asking a woman why she is wearing white to her second wedding. Or asking someone why they want to get a driver's license because they don't own a car yet. Seriously, people!

6. What is he/she?

Ummm... human form of a male/female during the daylight hours, but after dark, it goes back to it's original form of a three-headed alien serpent. We can't feed it after midnight either. Next question?

7. Do you know who it's real parents are?

Well, seeing as we're pretty fake people, it could be anyone, really. (And by the way, do you make a practice of referring to a human child as "it"?)

8. Don't you wish you'd been able to get pregnant?

No, I wouldn't want to endure the miracle of life and feel my child grow and move inside my body and build a bond with them. That would be so icky.

9. Wow, it doesn't look anything like you!

No!? Really!? You don't say. Shocker right there I tell ya. Must be defective. Remind me to call the manufacturer in the morning and see if there is a warranty.

10. So, what are you going to do with him/her now?

Oh, I dunno. I'll just leave him/her in the corner of the solarium by the ficus for the next few months and see what happens.

I swear. Some people think that it's alright to ask adoptive parents questions like these right flat out. It's not, it's really not ok. It's rude and intrusive. It's just as rude and intrusive as walking up to a pregnant woman and putting your hands on her belly without asking first, although an awful lot of people do that as well! And asking when she's due, boy or girl? Was it a natural conception? Will she have a natural birth? And yet so many people do that every day too.

It's not ok for either of those scenarios, and you as unwilling recipient of all this unwanted attention, do have the right to tell people that it's none of their business.

But, be prepared, you will be asked these types of

questions, and more. It will never cease to amaze you how intrusive and rude some people will be.

10. MY FAMILY IS SPLIT ON THE ISSUE

This is where things can get very touchy for some families. If you are one of the lucky ones whose extended family is completely understanding and in agreement with your plans to adopt, that is fantastic! You've got this covered, and congratulations to having such a wonderful support system around you. Hang on to them like the most precious gem you have ever had, because that is exactly what they are.

There are some that have, as I did, amazing family and friends that are willing to go on the journey with you, and help you along the way. They will be by your side through the good, the bad, and the ugly. And trust me when I say, there will be plenty of all of it.

And a great support circle is the best thing any adoptee or adoptive parents could hope for.

For others, it's not that easy.

There are some families that are against this issue, and others that are not exactly against it, but not very supportive of your decision to adopt. Some have families where both the husband and wife's families are not accepting of adoption. That's where really tough decisions have to be made because while there is the possibility that to fulfill your dream of being parents, you may have to sacrifice your own family for it.

You may have to come to terms that they will never accept it, and that you will be forever shunned for your decision. And if that happens, you need to be able to take ownership of that and make sure that the child you bring into your life, your home and your heart must never ever feel that this is any fault of their own. Because it's not. That family will miss out greatly on the joy of a child because of their narrow minded views and inability to be open and understanding. They will ultimately lose out in the long run.

There are other families where, let's say, the wife's side of the family is all for it and loves the idea and can't wait to welcome any new addition to their family. They will welcome him or her with open arms and treat them their entire lives like they were born naturally of their own flesh and blood and that is the best scenario anyone can hope for. Everyone lives in love and harmony as a family. As families ideally should.

Then there is the father's side, that isn't in agreement at all. Maybe they believe that if you're not meant to have children, then you shouldn't because that is what is meant to be, or, maybe they just feel that if the child isn't of the natural bloodline to the family that they aren't "worthy" so to speak, of carrying the family name. I have even heard of some families comparing taking in an adopted child to taking in a stray dog off the street. Yes, some people do think that way and do make that comparison.

Let's begin with discussing the family that isn't thrilled with the idea of adoption, but not exactly against it.

Chances are, they're just apprehensive because as a natural human emotion, people are often afraid of the unknown. They may be skeptical that the child will have something "wrong" with it, or grow up to be a "bad" child, or that they will look so much different from the adoptive parents that it will be very obvious to others that the child doesn't "belong" to them. Maybe they are ok with the idea, but want to keep it private so no one knows about it. Maybe they see it as a fault of theirs that one of their children can't conceive. There are so many reasons that the adoptive grandparents, aunts and uncles may be a bit uncertain about this process.

Maybe they fear questions, or ridicule. For themselves, for their children planning to adopt, and finally, for the child they will be bringing in.

Ultimately, the decision to adopt is yours as parents alone, no one else's. No one should make you feel bad or guilt you into not adopting. That needs to be said straight off.

There may be people in your life that will try to deter you with these questions, comments and ideas. They may even flat out tell you it's a bad idea. They will try to convince you of all the reasons you shouldn't do it. Reasons such as the child might be "bad", they might have learning disabilities, they might be sick, they might have a life threatening disease you won't know about until it's too late, and so on, and so on.

What they fail to remember is that even with a natural child, they may still have behavioural issues, or learning disabilities, or not look like the parents! Maybe there are traits in the ancestry that will be more dominant. Maybe a natural child could have physical impairments, birth defects, or even conditions like Down's Syndrome. Many families that aren't accepting of the idea of adoption because of those reasons I listed above often forget that those things are also possible with any natural child as well.

Maybe they worry about how the topic of adoption will be approached by the adoptive parents as well as received by the adopted child. This is why I covered the topic of honesty and communication first before anything else. It's only when and how you communicate that will determine what the outcome might be and how the child may receive the information.

More often than not, I have heard and found that when a family is "on the fence" so to speak about the adoption, once they see the excitement and happiness of the adoptive parents over it, it becomes very contagious. The family generally starts to get excited about it too, and then once that beautiful bundle of joy comes through the door, everyone succumbs to the miracle of a new baby, and it's quickly forgotten how apprehensive they first were. It's usually fairly smooth sailing from that point on in terms of how the family will treat the child in time.

Then, there are also the families that are completely against the idea of adoption no matter which way you present it. This is where you as adoptive parents have a lot of soul searching to do and some very hard decisions to make. And especially in these cases, they can't be made lightly. The last thing you want to do is make a rash decision and adopt out of determination, or even spite. This will create more of a rift than you (and your child) may be able to handle. This can be a major cause for resentment between existing family members, as well as cause resentment towards the child that you are adopting. Not only from the other family members, but possibly, from the parents as well.

The important thing that needs to be remembered is that the child didn't ask to be adopted any more that he or she would ask to be born. This is a conscious decision that you and your partner will be making so you need to be sure of what you are doing, that it is for the right reasons, and that no matter how it goes between family members, the child can not be held responsible for the decisions that you made before he or she even existed.

My one side of the family was fantastic. They welcomed the adoption process with open arms and open hearts. There was never any different treatment between the children that were cousins of the ones born naturally from other couples in the family. We were all treated as equals as if we were all legitimate children from the same blood lines.

My grandparents (and parents) treated each child, biological or not completely and one hundred percent equal. What one got on one of their many vacations as souvenirs, the other of the same gender got the same.

For example, when we were younger, the girls got dolls from each country or destination, the exact same doll, but in different colours, or different outfits/hair colour etc... the boys got t-shirts the same in their sizes but different colour or logo. Never, ever were any of us treated different from the other. When we got older, if one of my grandparents paid a bill, let's say, for one of us, then the other ones would be given the equivalent in either cash or one of their bills paid of the same value. Everything was equal. They believed firmly in being honest and equal even when they could have easily not told anyone that they had helped out one of us.

We never had to worry about being left out, treated

different, or being made to feel different. We were treated so well and I have such wonderful memories of both of my grandparents on the one side. They would only talk about the adoption if we wanted to. If it was never mentioned, then it was never talked about.

When I adopted my one daughter five years before I had my biological one, and also welcomed her older sister who was 10 years her senior into my life, my grandfather had already passed away, but, my grandmother was so amazing with her as well as her older sister. She called them her granddaughters, and they called her Great Grandma. Again, she was more than happy and willing to welcome another life, another child, both of them, into her life as her own flesh and blood. My grandparents helped teach me, as did my adoptive parents, that love is love. No matter where it comes from, or who it comes from, as long as it's unselfish, genuine, and unconditional, then that was all that mattered.

I remember when I was younger, I was talking to my grandmother about being adopted, and I remember her telling me something that always stuck in my mind. In my early teens, I mentioned that I would like to one day maybe meet my real mother.

She said "well, if that's what you'd like to do, then you do what you feel you must if you think that will help you. We will still support you and be your grandparents, but whatever you think is best for you." I wouldn't have traded them for anything. They were truly the best grandparents any kid could wish for.

Then there was the other side of it. The other side of the family that was not so accepting of the idea, or of my parents for doing it, or of me as the adopted child.

There was always a huge rift between my parents and that side of the family because of it. There was always a very uneasy feeling in the air whenever the family got together. There was always a feeling of unease, that I was being watched, that I was being scrutinized, and analyzed. There was never any real acceptance, and it was obvious.

It was obvious in the way I was spoken to, the way I was treated, in the way I was included, but in a very secluded way. It was as if I was kept at an arm's length, and never really welcomed, but never outwardly shunned. I was treated politely, but in a very sarcastic way. There were always little side comments that were, as I look back, more directed at my parents than at me.

The comments were more geared to hurt them than me. If they ended up hurting me in the process, it seems to me looking back, that they didn't care. Indeed, it was more successful if I did understand the comment, or the reason for the comment. If I was hurt as well and that would be a double bonus for them that they not only hurt my feelings but hurt my parents too. They were not very kind people, and only made it look like they were kind in actions only. Everything they did was for appearances sake, and certainly not because they cared to or wanted to. Over time, they made that abundantly clear.

When it came to birthdays, all the girls were made handmade dresses, for instance. The other girls would have unbelievably beautiful dresses that were full of everything little girls loved - lace, multiple layers and ruffles, and when you spun around, it was a huge flair. You could see the craftsmanship in my grandmother's work. It was beautiful, flawless. And always what every little girl wanted and dreamed of. The girls would go crazy for them and there would be hugs and kisses and always the same responses in reply, "Oh I'm so glad you like it! I worked so hard to find exactly what you wanted."

Not mine. Mine were still made with the same skill, but you could see that the minimal amount of effort was put into it. They were very simple, and plain. Only 1 type of fabric with a small lace trim around the bottom of I was lucky. Usually it was only a ribbon trim and there was rarely enough material to leave me enough room to walk in it, let alone spin and have it flare out like theirs did.

No way. That would never happen. And I always heard the same comments after I would gush about how much I loved it, which was said with a dismissive wave of the hand, "oh, I had some scrap material on hand that I had enough to make a dress out of."

Family get togethers like Christmas were especially awkward. They were dreaded immensely not just by me but by my poor parents. They waited in anticipation to see if this was the year things would finally be equal. It never happened. They also, ironically, waited to see if this would be the year the straw broke the camel's back.

The last horrible Christmas we had with them, was the one. And I say the last, because after this particular Christmas, my parents said they would no longer do a family Christmas with the entire family, but we would just visit on our own sometime during the season without everyone else there.

It was heartbreaking. I was 10 years old. We anticipated as usual, a nice big dinner, and then afterwards, we all went to the basement to play pool while my grandmother cleaned up the dinner dishes, and then have dessert, and then after that, back to the basement to exchange gifts. This was the usual ritual. There was one really big gift in the corner, and no one knew who it was for. There were lots of gifts, as usual. Some big, some small, some medium sized. So, we all sat down and waited for our grandfather to start handing out the gifts. One by one, I watched the other two girls open pretty gift after pretty gift, and then, they each opened up their medium sized gifts, to reveal the prized porcelain dolls that we all collected. They were stunning. All Victorian dressed, with long curls, velvet and lace dressed, with hats and umbrellas. Each one's hair matched their new owner's hair colour.

I waited in anticipation praying that I got one with blue eyes and blonde hair in a pretty dress like those.

Nope.

I got a simple Barbie doll. I was so disappointed. But I was also still grateful because I had a little barbie collection that I could happily add her to. My next gift was a very tiny plastic upright piano music box. When you opened the little lid, it played music. I liked music. But then, I thought, maybe, just maybe, seeing as they had gotten so much more than I did, and much nicer gifts, that possibly that last big gift in the back corner just might possibly be for me.

Boy, was I ever wrong. How could I have been so silly to think such a ridiculous thing? The other two girls were called over and told to unwrap the last huge gift, that was a gift for both of them. I held my breath in anticipation as to what it could possibly be.

It was the biggest and most spectacular dollhouse any little girl could dream about. It was fully carpeted, wallpapered, furnished, artwork on the walls, little mirrors, tiny books on bookshelves, had working lights and even a doorbell! I stared at it in disbelief. I looked over to my mom and dad, and they immediately saw the hurt and disappointment in my eyes. My Dad called me over to come sit on his lap because he knew that I needed to be comforted. I sat on his lap for the rest of the evening while my mother stroked my hair and told me not to worry about it, that they would take care of everything, and to just be polite, say thank you and that we would be getting ready to leave soon.

When we left that night, and I cried all the way home. I cried myself to sleep. I heard my parents talking about it that night, and they were so very upset about it and the way I was treated. I refused to let them see how much they had hurt me while we were still there so it all let go once we left. I was so confused as to why I was treated so differently and why they could be so mean as to give such expensive and beautiful things to them and not to me as well. I knew right then and there that I was different. That I would be forever different. That I would be treated differently by them for the rest of my life. My poor parents felt so bad about it. They promised me that one day they would be able to make it right.

My parents were true to their word. We never went back after that for any family gatherings. We would stop by on Christmas or on my grandparents birthdays just to "keep the peace" as my father called it. We always brought them small gifts but never expected any in return. And rarely got any anyways. My grandfather was always very welcoming to us, and kind, but you could tell that he always tried to stay out of it and stay neutral. When he passed away, I never went back after that. There was never any point and we all knew it. My Dad went to see his mother on her birthday, Mother's day, or Christmas, but we never went again. He didn't blame us. He said he would rather just go himself than have the headache that went along with it if we all went. He was the eternal diplomat.

Over the years, my Dad always felt so bad about it. Then, one day, out in the back yard, when I was in my late teens, my dad built a shed out back, and made it look like a little house. Complete with little porch, windows, and curtains! Just for me. I was absolutely thrilled. He said that it was mine to use as my own little life size dollhouse. I could use it as a reading room or whatever I wanted. I told him I loved it and I wanted him to use it for his things but I absolutely love it. It still stands in the backyard to this day. I cherish it with all my heart. He swore that he would make sure that I was never made to feel like that ever again.

When I took on the role of mom to my hubby's two year old daughter who didn't have a mother, my parents also welcomed her with open arms and treated her like she was their own grandchild. They made sure that even she got her own dollhouse to play with. They wanted to make sure she was loved like a family and that she would never be treated different or be made to feel insignificant like I was. She had an older sister that was 10 years her senior, as I mentioned, and they still treated her like family as well. Of course, things were always given to her as well, according to her age, and they always did their best to make her feel included and loved as well. They even wanted them to call them Grammie and Grampy.

I was thrilled with this as I was told that the chances of my being able to have children of my own weren't great. I was quite happy being mom to her and a mom figure to her older sister. We were a happy little family. They loved and adored the girls with all their hearts, and they doted on them any every chance they got.

One of the first things my Mom and Dad did, was buy everything needed to make the little one her very own dollhouse. And it was a BIG one. My dad built it with odds and ends of wood, fabric, bought some dollhouse furniture, and others he made himself. Little couches and chairs, tiny clippings out of magazines for artwork to hang on the walls, and every room was carpeted and wallpapered. The only thing this dollhouse didn't have, was lights. Unfortunately, he couldn't figure out how to do that part of it, but really wanted to. We told him it was ok that he didn't because this was even better than the original he was trying to duplicate. This one was hand made, with love and pride, and that more than made up for no working electricity. He made sure that she would never have to experience what I did.

Three years later, I was miraculously pregnant with

my daughter. My parents were over the moon excited. They, again, took her on with love and adoration and doted on her just the same as the others. Because the age gap between the little one and my daughter was only 5 years, it was fairly easy to do the same for them as my one set of grandparents did. They were equal with everything. If one got something, then so did the other. If one got three new outfits, then so did the other. If one got a new toy, then so did the other. The older one got something equal in value, but geared towards her age instead.

My parents were very strong believers in everyone being treated equal. They never wanted any child to feel left out, feel like they were valued less, or loved less than another. They went out of their way to ensure that it never happened.

My only suggestions to dealing with a family split on the issue as we had to, or even if they are completely opposed to it, is to make sure that the child never feels as if it's his or her fault. Ultimately, you will do whatever it is that you feel is best, but the last thing you want is for your child/children to get caught in the middle of it. They are already going to have feelings of naturally doubting their self worth at some point, as I said it is very common and very normal, without having to have that double-whammy of having complete strangers that are supposed to be family now not want them too. That will take an irreparable hit to their already fragile ego.

As I already mentioned before, this is where really tough decisions have to be made because there is the possibility that to fulfill your dream of being parents, you may have to sacrifice your own family to do it. You may have to come to terms that they will never accept it, and that you will be forever shunned by some, or all of your family for your decision. And if that happens, you need to be able to take ownership of that and make sure that the child you bring into your life, your home and your heart must never ever feel that this is any fault of their own. Because, it's not. That family will miss out greatly on the joy of a child because of their narrow minded views and inability to be open and understanding. They will ultimately lose out in the long run.

Yes, sometimes when that new bundle of smiles and drool comes into everyone's lives, he or she will captivate their hearts and all trepidation will be forgotten in an instant, sometimes not. So while an open and honest discussion with family is always highly recommended, but you should never base your final decisions solely on what they think.

If you believe in your heart that this is the right step for you to take, then you make the best educated decision that you can make. Just always keep in mind that your decisions will always have a negative or positive reaction no matter which way you choose. And, if you should choose to include a child in your life, that all those negative or positive reactions will also impact the life of the child as well.

You always need to do whatever is best for you, and no one can tell you what to do, you have to decide for yourself, and live with the decision that you make for yourself, as well as for that child.

11. *WHERE MY JOURNEY HAS TAKEN ME*

My journey has been a very interesting one. I have gone through so many emotions from sadness; to self pity; self loathing; to hating my birth mother; to yearning for her; to ambivalence; determination, and the list goes on and on.

Not one of these emotions, or any of the million I have had in between, are any more right or wrong than the other. Every single thought and emotion I have had about this whole process of gathering my birth information, to gaining my birth mother's information, to writing this book, are all valid in their own right.

Even now, at 41 years old, I just applied for my original birth certificate. Something I never thought to get. It was suggested to me by a friend who runs a Search Trace Locate company that assists in locating birth families. She is also an admin on the Facebook Support Group that I started in the called Adoptees/Birth Families GTA Resource - Toronto, Ontario, Canada Area ONLY. We started talking one night because of a post someone had made and it turned into a private conversation about identifying information and non identifying information and original registration of live birth. She asked if I had mine and I honestly had no idea what she was talking about. I didn't even know you could get a copy of that. I knew you could get a copy of your adoption order, and you could get a "long version" copy of your birth certificate, that, as a rule, will have your mother and father's names listed on it. But, being adopted, I figured it was pointless because all it would have was my adoptive parents info on it. And I was right.

However, you could apply for a copy of your original registration of live birth. I had no idea. I was shocked. She told me that generally, as long as you fill out the exact form required from the government, you could get this, and many times, more often than not, it would have the address of the birth mother at the time of the live birth.

And it did.

Here's where it gets REALLY strange.

The place where she lived when I was born, my adoptive parents were living only about 5 blocks away from her just the year before! They moved to a town about a half hour drive north of there just after putting in their adoption request for a little girl.

And my husband grew up 2 blocks away from her! The chances of that are unbelievably rare. He thinks he may know that family by means of association, but, unfortunately, that house has long been demolished and a new residential area put in many years ago. However, he still has many old high school connections from that area and time, and is pretty sure he can find out more information as he talks to old friends over social media. He's checking around to find out what he can in the meantime.

So, when it came time to open that letter with my live birth registration in it, I wasn't sure what to expect.

It was a little scary, to be honest. Even though I already knew my birth name, and my mother's name, it was still almost terrifying to know that I was going to know just that little bit more. What that little bit more was, I wasn't sure. I would have to wait to get the paper and see what exactly it said. I was one of the very lucky people that had applied for all of my information prior to 2008 when the laws changed and they no longer gave out identifying information after that. I was very lucky, and very grateful that I applied for it when I did.

When I told my mom that I was applying for it, she was excited for me. She was genuinely hoping it had a little more information for me that I maybe didn't already have, something that I maybe didn't know yet. Another piece to the little puzzle.

I always kept my parents informed of what I was doing and when. They always knew exactly what was going on, because this would have impact on their lives as well. I was their daughter, their little girl, their baby. I never wanted to keep them out of the loop when it came to doing anything with my adoption information.

When I was asked to be on a couple of newscasts in regards to adoption, and the adoption laws, and how they affected adoptees, I gladly accepted. I invited my parents to come along and be part of it. Some of it was even filmed in my home and again, I wanted them there to be a part of it. Because it had everything to do with them as well as me. I was sought out a couple of times because of the adoption groups and support groups that I run on Facebook that are quite busy for the Toronto GTA, have quite a large population, and are very busy and active.

Finally, it arrived. I waited until I was home from the

mailbox to open it. I actually waited quite a while. For some strange reason, I just couldn't bring myself to open it right away. I was scared to death! Why? Why was I scared? What did I have to be afraid of? It's just a piece of paper. I had no idea what I was afraid of, I just knew that I was afraid.

I sat down, with my husband, and finally opened it.

When I pulled out the paper, I literally lost my breath. My stomach dropped, and I felt a huge wash of emotion come over me. I was overwhelmed by an emotional overload. I felt every possible emotion there is that any person can feel, all at the exact same time. Overlapping each other like waves rushing in on a beach.

There was my birth name, and my adopted name in brackets, side by side. Oh my gosh. I had already been picked for my parents before I was even born. Someone had already decided that I was to go to them right after I was born.

Then it really hit me. Hard.

Harder than I had expected it would. I honestly thought that I was prepared for pretty much anything at this point and that I had already experienced every possible emotion that there was for experience about this topic. This is where that old saying rings true that you always think you are prepared for something, and no matter how much you prepare, you never really are.

Things I already knew were suddenly truth and staring me right in the face. It was very bizarre because even though I knew from many discussions twenty years ago with the worker that was helping me get together all my non identifying and identifying information, that my mother had already decided long before I was born that she was putting me up for adoption, and that she was "ambivalent in her decision" to put me up for adoption as it was so plainly stated in my papers, there it was in black and white. The reality that my mother had made the decision to give me away. And it upset me a lot. I wasn't prepared for that. I was not prepared in any way for the things I was feeling. It was just a piece of paper solidifying what I already knew, so it should be no big deal, right?

Oh, but it was. I was honestly saddened by the reality of it. I knew my mother's name, and I knew I was adopted, but there it was, in her own handwriting. Her handwriting. My mother wrote that. She wrote her name. She signed me away. She signed me over the same way you sign the back of your car's ownership when you sell it to someone else.

That is how I first took it. I immediately felt like I was 10 years old again, sitting in my grandmother's basement at Christmas, being shunned by someone who should have loved me but didn't.

I sat there staring at this piece of paper, choking back tears. Wishing desperately that my father were still alive so I could show it to him. He would be able to make sense of it all for me. He would be able to talk me through it the way no one else ever could, not even my Mom. He just had a certain way of wording things that made it easier to dissect, digest, and understand.

But, this time, he wasn't here and I would have to sort through the feelings on this on myself. I sat with my husband and talked to him about it, and how I was feeling. At first, he didn't really understand my reaction because, just as I had thought, he believed I was prepared for this. He said he was shocked by my reaction because of two reasons. The first being that it was "just a piece of paper" and the second, because I knew it was coming because I had applied for it and had been waiting and checking the mail daily for it's arrival.

I honestly didn't know how to respond at first to the "just a piece of paper" comment. I was immediately angry, offended, and hurt that he didn't understand it and that he had trivialized the whole thing by that one insensitive comment. I had to stop and bite my tongue and think before speaking. Before letting my hurt feelings get the better of me. I stopped and thought. I thought about this book, and the reasons for writing it. I completely, at that point, understood all of my reasons for writing it.

Because of my hopes of helping not only the adoptee, and adoptive parents understand all of the reasons we all feel what we may feel, act the ways we might act, lash out in the ways we might, and get frustrated with how we feel and why, but also get frustrated with others not understanding the reasons either. To help the siblings, aunts & uncles, grandparents, and even spouses better understand it too.

After processing what he had said, I realized he didn't mean for it to be insensitive, or sound insensitive. He didn't mean to trivialize it, he just simply didn't understand it. And, for him, it was a simple, harmless question. When I explained to him how it made me feel and why, and how his reaction and comments towards me hurt my feelings, he understood much clearer why I had the reactions that I did. And in explaining it to him, I found it was also very therapeutic for me as well. It was good to verbalize and not internalize it. I had a lot of revelations in that one moment of conversation about all of this, and these issues, topics, feelings and emotions. That was, for the moment, the last piece to the closure puzzle. It solidified the "I'm adopted, I'm someone, I'm no one, I'm me, but I'm not" train of thought and emotions roller coaster that I have been on.

I believe that we need to do these things in very specific and deliberate steps in order to not have a complete and utter emotional overload and meltdown. There is no way that anyone can possibly take on all the information all at once, digest, and process it in any semblance of organization or understanding.

The process of writing this book has not only been for myself, but for so many others that just have no idea where to begin with something that seems so easy to understand - feelings. Most people understand why they are angry and who they are angry with. Adoptees don't have that understanding or that ability to understand fully because we don't even know who we are, let alone who the responsible parties, the birth parents, are. How do you know what you're mad about when you don't know who you are mad at to begin with?

This is why I say so often that communication is key because, without it, you can so easily get lost in your own thoughts, ideas and opinions that you can very easily lose track of yourself and what it is that you are trying to accomplish, whether it be just gaining answers, or figuring out who you are and where you came from. Some people are just happy knowing the mere basics of their situations, and others need more. Everyone is different. But, when you are communicating with any one person, or multiple people in your support circles, you will find that many questions about who you think you are and how you feel and why are answered much more easily than if you bottle everything up and keep it to yourself, and internalizing it all.

When you speak out loud, and brainstorm, chances are that one question asked, or answered, will bring up another, and another, and another, and sometimes even questions that you hadn't even thought of yet. Sometimes the brainstorming will help you to better understand how you feel, and when you talk to other adoptees, you will find that you are not alone, and not the only one that feels the way you do.

Until I really sat and talked with my husband about how I was feeling and why, he didn't really understand it either. That was my fault for not discussing it with him, or including him in my discussions because I didn't think he would understand it. I didn't give him that benefit of the doubt, or that respect. Up until the day that original copy of my birth certificate came, I had only ever talked to other adoptees, or my parents about my feelings and my emotional turmoil. I realized that, and started to open up more to him, and the more he could get a grasp on what was going on in my head over the whole thing. And the more I realized he didn't have a true understanding of my side of it, even when I thought he did!

I never really once thought to actually TALK to him about it. I just always figured he "got it" and "got me" and "understood me" without actually TELLING him what I thought, and why. I knew what I understood, and what I "get", but he also never thought to talk to me about it because he didn't think I'd want to, or else I would have brought it up to him. He didn't think I DID think about it every day, and figured I didn't want to.

That's where adoptees are very different. We think about it constantly. Even when we don't mean to, or want to. It just happens. A sappy family gathering at Christmas commercial on tv can trigger it. Watching a family outing at the park can trigger it. Hearing a little one call out in glee for their mother picking their child up from school can trigger it. Birthdays definitely trigger it!

In talking with him about all of this, he asked what my next step was. I said I wasn't really sure. I had reached out to a friend in one of my support groups that runs a Search Trace Locate company, and we were talking about seeing what she could do to possibly find my mother now that we had that little bit of information that I was previously lacking.

My main motivation for wanting to locate her at this stage of my life is more for the medical information of my family history that I will need to pass on to my own daughter now. There are many medical issues that I have currently that could potentially be hereditary, and there are some that were listed in the non-identifying information that I was given that will be of use to her later on in life as well. Unless I locate her and actually speak to her, there is no way I will ever truly know.

This also opens up a whole other can of worms. At this point, I am really not sure if I am looking to form a relationship with her. What if we make contact with her, and she decides that she wants to also get to know me, and meet with me? Am I ready for that? I really don't know. That is a huge step that I'm not sure that I want to make. Maybe my opinion of that will clarify, or solidify once the opportunity presents itself, if it does. You can say you think you know what you might do, but once you're in that situation, you never really do know what you will do.

What if she decides that there will be no contact in any way, shape, or form and she says she isn't even going to forward any medical history to me either. That happens all the time. Then, of course, what if she says yes to forwarding medical info but says no contact otherwise? Then that will pose a real problem also because there will obviously be questions about it that I won't get answers to either. I think that would be the hardest option if it were to happen.

As much as I may think I am ready for any or all of these scenarios, I know deep down that, really, I'm not, and won't be when any of them happen. I would only be fooling myself to think otherwise. This is the point where you just have to take things very slowly, and one step at a time, as you can handle it. Don't ever take on too much, especially mentally or emotionally. The only person that is going to pay for that in a negative and destructive way, is you.

My own search demonstrates another part that you need to remember: These things take time. It isn't a TV movie where you reach legal age and find your birth parents in a matter of weeks or months and everything's hunky dory by the end of year. It can take many years, decades, to not only sort out your own feelings but to find the information and attempt to reach out. Searching is an emotionally complex process, as is the actual search for information and every time you acquire that extra piece, you may need time to stop and reevaluate your emotional data bank. There's nothing wrong with this, give yourself as much time as you need. Don't allow anyone to push you and, more importantly, don't push yourself into doing things before you're ready.

And, if you have children, as I do, that know that I am adopted, then, of course, they will also feel the effects of whatever it is that you are going through. They're also going to have questions. Whenever my kids have asked me anything about being adopted, I always answer as best as I can in ways they can understand, what it is, what it's all about and how it makes me feel.

I am very lucky that my one girl I have adopted has a much better understanding of me, and of herself as well because of all of this. She and I have had many conversations about my being adopted, and my adopting her. I can talk to her on a level that I can't talk to my biological daughter on because she is biological. It's a little harder for her to understand because of that, but, at the same time, oddly enough, also understands it completely as well.

She understands my being adopted by her

grandparents because she knows that I have adopted her sister, and the reasons that I did. So, the two situations hand in hand have enabled her to have a better grasp on it than many kids would of her age. That, coupled with the fact that we are a very open and honest family unit, we will talk very openly and freely about anything and everything. There's nothing the girls can't talk to me, or their dad, or even their grandparents about.

When their grandpa, my father, was alive, each of them would spend endless hours just talking about anything and everything. And they still do with their grandma, as well as both their dad and I . Life, families, school, growing up, the birds and the bees, adoption, siblings, you name it. There has never been, nor ever will be any topic that is off limits with us.

When my kids found out that I was writing this book, they were very interested in it, and asked many questions. All of which I answered as best as I could, and, ironically, gave me extra things to write about that hadn't come into my mind yet. Another example of why communication is so important. When they found out that I had gotten a copy of my original birth certificate, of course, they were both very excited to see it, and see what it looked like "way back then". They were very surprised to see, as I was, that it included my birth name and my adopted name. They are very interested in what my next steps are, and how this will all work itself out.

Until they asked me a few days after getting my original birth certificate, if I was going to try and find my mother, I never really thought about it seriously. And that was when I decided that now was as good a time as any to reach out to my support group and not only get feedback, but, possibly, some affirmation that I was still "normal" in what I was thinking and feeling about it all. When I brought it to the attention of my Search Team, I was told that ultimately, it was my decision, but in the best interests of my medical information, and my biological daughter, I had a responsibility to be as informed for my health future, as well as for hers. And they're right of course. As long as I make that step towards communication, and attempt to get the medical answers that we need, even if I don't get them, at least the effort was made and I can rest easy that I did what I could. Because, after all, as the adoptee, it's generally forgotten that although we are entitled to answers, and have a right to answers, we also ultimately have the right to choose what answers we want. I have the right to accept the medical answers, but also the right to refuse the relationship and contact option. But that is something that has to be decided when that opportunity presents itself, and can not be definitively made without being first placed in that scenario with that option on the table at that time.

Rash, uneducated decisions will, more often than not, turn into regrets.

Regrets are the beginning of a downward spiral of

nothing but negativity in depression, anger, loathing, resentment, and hate. Whatever decision I make moving forward, I need to make sure it is one that I won't regret.

In the event that my biological mother wants to meet, even just once, I can honestly say I do believe that I would take that opportunity. Even if it's to only meet once, I think it would help make an educated decision in deciding if a relationship is something I want to pursue or not. What if that is the only opportunity I ever get? What if I say no, and then change my mind later, but it's too late and now she has changed her mind. Then what? No one wins, we all lose.

For me, I guess the journey will have to continue in another chapter of another book.

Right now, I'm still searching. Searching for answers as to who I am, who she is, where I came from, and where I should head. Right now, I'm still me, but I'm still not. And until that day comes where we meet face to face, and have some questions answered, I don't think I will ever truly feel like "myself" or know exactly who I am.

I have to admit, being an adoptee is a very interesting thing to be. And that's exactly what it is. It's a being, it's almost like it's a "thing", a separate entity in your life. It's a way of life for so many of us. It can take hold of your life and turn it upside down if you let it. Who knows where the end of my journey will be at this point in my life? I can only hope for the best possible outcome.

All I do know is that it has been a very interesting journey. It has led me to meet some very fantastic people through my support groups, has lead me to appear on tv and try to have some small voice for the adoptees and pleading with all biological mothers to please, have some compassion when it comes to meeting your child you put up for adoption.

Please try to understand that they are trying to make sense of their lives, who they are, and understand your decisions.

It has lead me in many positive ways as well. It has allowed me to have a wonderful relationship with my adoptive parents, and a grasp on the tolerance required for the family members that have shunned them, and me. I don't hate them for it; I don't begrudge them for it. They're ignorant of the processes of human nature because they are selfish. That's not a speculation. That's a fact. Love has no boundaries, and love has no labels. If those people can't love unconditionally, then I pity them because they are the ones that are truly missing out on so much they aren't even aware of. They just don't know any better, and some just don't care to.

Surround yourselves with the ones that do, and you'll be more content in your own skin than they ever will be. And, that ultimately, is where you will have the upper hand, and where you will come out the winner.

I have learned to be able to have open and honest communication with not only my friends, but my family, and my children. I believe this makes me not only a better person, but a better daughter, a better wife, and a better mother.

This journey has also enabled me to do something I never thought I would accomplish. I have been able to complete this book.

Writing this book alone has been a journey in itself. A very positive journey. It has enabled me to be able to be able to really sit, and look within myself for answers to questions that only I, myself, have the answers to. I have been able to analyze certain things about myself that I wasn't able to before. I actually have a better understanding of myself. And I have a better understanding of others as well. I see anything that you do that is positive and benefits yourself and others in a positive way mentally and emotionally a very good thing that should be explored and nurtured.

I know I have been able to help myself in writing this book, and if I am able to help even one other person have a better understanding of who they are, who they might be, or even pointed them in a direction that helps them, then I have achieved what my ultimate goal in writing this book.

My journey is mine, and mine alone. I choose which baggage to carry along with me, and I choose who I want to bring along on the ride with me. I decide to take the scenic route, or the express route. Either way, I'll get where I need to go at some point. And, so will you.

Each of us have our journey to make, and we will all make them. In our own good time, in our own ways. No two ways will be exactly alike, no two ways will turn out exactly the same, and no two destinations will be exactly the same. The only similarity that we all share that is exactly the same, is that although we are all headed in the same direction, looking at the same type of scenery go by, but we are all looking at it at different times, in different seasons, with different baggage, and different traveling companions.

But, we are all ultimately all riding the same train.

Made in the USA
Charleston, SC
07 May 2016